To Joe

Unfinished Times

Brian Moore

Best Wishes

ORIGINAL WRITING

ISBN: 978-1-908282-91-0

A CIP catalogue for this book is available from the National Library.

Published by Original Writing Ltd., Dublin, 2011.

Printed by Cahills Printers Ltd

For my Mother and Father Liam and Eileen Moore.

The Love that is given and received,
the flesh and blood, the breath and bone,
are ties that bind us to this life.
When the spirit is set free,
to where it wanders,
no one knows.

Acknowledgements

Tom Collins
Cover Design Concept, and Back Cover Photo.

Siobhan Moore
For Constant Love and Support.

Thanks to John, Robert, and Kevin.

Special Thanks to
Joseph and Olivia Moore,
Maire and Vincent Nolan.

Introduction

I first began writing poetry when I was sixteen, back in 1972. The poems were written in school copy books, which I titled and kept, some of the titles are referred to in this selection, ie Poems from Love in a Mist, Mystic Moments, The poems were written once, never gone back over or re edited. In 1973 I had two poems published in the first ever school literary magazine, in Oatlands college Stillorgan, this gave me the confidence to keep writing, however, things began to fizzle out in the eighties after I got married, there was not enough time to write, with career, and the raising of two small boys, it was a hectic time.

Towards the end of the decade I decided to write again, after several attempts I gave up.Empty pages are like looking at a map, you see the roads, the towns, the cities, but the car will not start. In the early nineties I began another copy book, which was titled Unfinished Times, and thats exactly what it ended up as, with only a couple of entries.

In the Spring Of 2009 my good friend Pete Ryan gave me a copy of the school magazine from 1973, that stoked the creative juices, So I got all the old copies, picked out what I thought were the best, and restructured them, some of them I did not change at all. I decided to write some new pieces, to include, which turned out better than I thought they would. Notably, The title poem, and The Bitter and the Sweet. I enjoyed the challenge, and decided to call the final result, UNFINISHED TIMES, after so many failed attempts, and my obsession with time and its many symphonies that we have to weave our life's dance to.

Contents

Unfinished Times

All the young dancers

The party girls shop until they drop,
hopping from one fickle purchase to the next,
endless hours in preparation party mode,
still they look the same,
its all part of the game,
another never ending cycle, of ritualistic
indulgence, in the sweetened years of youth.

The alpha males dance in groups, posing, and
posturing, like gorillas in the wild,
boys high on every thing, that might lead
to some romantic interlude with one of
those exotic party dolls,
The night moves along,
the DJ plays the songs.
that swing and flow,
in this amazing show.

She's on the dance floor,
blinding disco lights show no mercy,
cascading multitudes of colours,
dance beside her, eyes glazed and blazing,
its a choreographed scene playing out.
The dancers are all in tune,
the beat, the heat,
the rhythm and the rhyme.
she knows the script,
it shines out through her.

He moves in for the final scene,
gracefully moving like a leopard stalking,
the party doll sways from side to side,
tottering on heels too high.
He catches her, they dance a magic pirouette,
around ,and around they dance as one,

Its the last chance dance and
Everyone is on the floor, the DJ pumps the music,
it takes off to a jet engine level,
an ear splitting sound reverberates
around the hall, back drafting off the walls.
This is the real deal,
The party doll, and the alpha male,
hamsters on the wheel.

The DJ is watching, from behind the decks,
his fingers moving, tweaking the levels,
one more notch, might blow the gig,
two shots like whip cracks, ricochet,
he sees the party doll spin and fall,
he sees her partner call out and fall,
a cigarette rolls carefully,
across the freshly polished floor.

There's blood blooming on her fine designer dress,
her face is pale, never again to feel his caress.
He lies beside her, eyes open but unseeing.
the DJ cuts the track, dims the lights.
fires one last blast from the smoke machine,
the camera slides behind the speaker stack,
and swivels out of sight.
Out of the swirling smoke,
the credits start to roll.

The people in the gallery begin to leave their seats,
satisfied, The film is over.
and all the young dancers are dead.

7th Nov 1974 / April 17th 2011.

Backroads

Tunes that remind me of you,
They take me back through time
on a purple ray of starlight
the years sprinkled with stardust,
those hidden fears and tears,
bubbling along like a babbling brook.

I see the Love in a Mist flower in
full bloom, bright smiling faces
dancing in a never ending pirouette,
I watch your silhouette, feel your embrace,
I can smell the garden in your hair.

The sweet face of youth defying all the odds
in that happy go lucky bubble of fun
Dancing in the disco, beyond reality
and the limits of restricted visions
kept me free, kept me warm
The keeper of my heart.

Beyond five years the memories become hazy,
times brittle hold loses its grip,
blurred faces wearing short trousers,
The faces are smiling, the sun is shining,
the tune is fading to a pale and crazy sound.
I cant see you anymore.

These twists continue to unfold
as the stories get told,
may I be so bold as to invite
you in from the cold,
and together we can stroll
down these Love in a Mist backroads.

1st Dec 1975

Dance Hall Graveyard

This is no place for you,
in this time that is yours,
the sounds are so loud and
the voices lost in there quest
to be found.
You've got to go now.

This is no town for you,
your Jane Birkin face
leaves not a trace,
in the blistering heat of
another nowhere day.

Your ice blue eyes cry
tears of stone,
and this flesh and bone
is pale and cold,
eyes caught in the harsh blinding
colours of spinning lights.

Alone on this river of life
too much time living the nightlife,
floating on towards the dawn,
playing the part of the sacrificial pawn.

Your Jane Birkin face,
leaves no trace,
as the neon graveyard lights
spit colours through the night.

Out in the bright light of the day,
your pretty face shows me the way.

4th October 1976

Drowning Pool

My life is a pool, sometimes dark and deep,
sometimes shallow and incomplete.
Ripples roll across it, in times of pain,
joy, or other emotional waves,
I'm drowning in this pool of life,
its just too deep at times, and the shallow
edges are lined with rocks.

Those around you, throw you things to cling to
like love and hate, and twigs of guilt,
you place them in the pocket of your past,
where they live separate lives in smaller pools.
I sink lower in my pool of life,
away from all the strife, where the waters are
tranquil, and the ripples of life wont disturb me,
Where the starving are all being fed, and the wars
of man are no more.

The pool of life is deep, and I long to see what lies
at the bottom, perhaps the wreckage of some previous
existence. Who knows? each cares for his own pool only.
My life is like a pool sometimes dark and deep,
but always incomplete,
I am but a twig floating on its surface,
drifting in the calm, hatches battened down,
Waiting for the storm.

2nd August 1992

Faded

Feeling more faded as these days of dreaming
slide into the realms of yesterday, on memories
the size of a postage stamp.
With faded jeans, and fading thoughts,
I wander down this road of life.
Twisting and turning around,
the torment and the strife.
Still the time flies by, blown along by the whispering wind.
You seem so far away, lost in a cavern of thought,
enveloped in your garden, where growth has all but stopped.
I'm dancing with you, to the treble and base of the heavens,
Now I'm falling, and falling, with nowhere to fall.
Its not your call, your a melody I just cant play.

Here in the silence of my room,
the colours gently fading,
first to grey and then to white,
The wisdom of your words bouncing in my head,
criss crossing over times elusive fields.
Many years too late.

All my songs are faded, my guitar is perfectly
tuned to the sound of silence,
loud and empty, racing toward the dawn.
Now the weeks are rolling on.
Does it matter anymore.
Feeling faded,
As these colours wash away,
like photographs gently fading.

14th September 1975

Francs Song

So play that Hendrix riff one more time Franc,
set out those bridges and leave them burning
behind you, what about all those if's and but's
and not forgetting the pesky little maybe's.
Ending in a musical cul de sac,
you couldn't play your way out of.

There's always a dream,
always a scheme,
my my my,
how quick the years fly by,
there's always a dream.

Too many bands, too many one night stands,
too many miles down those roads to nowheresville,
where the crowd stood around drunk while you
played your heart out,
your rock n roll years are fading fast,
and time a'int on your side,

There's always a dream,
always a scheme,
my my my,
how quick the years fly by,
there's always a dream.

Last I heard you were living in the Caribbean,
you got a winter gig playing in someone elses band,
now your strumming along singing someone elses songs,
and your dreams are like the forgotten songs of yesterday.
So play that Hendrix riff one more time Franc,
catch that midnight flight to another tinsel town,
where your band can play and the crowd all know your name.
and where guitar stars never seem to fade away.

There's always a dream
always a scheme,
my my my.
how quick the years fly by,
There's always a dream.
Your star was never far away.

(mid nineties)

Hard Love

She will always leave a chasm
no matter where you go,
the chasm is in your heart,
the one she put there, when she
flew away and left you
in the twilight zone.

Her tired body lovingly tied around you
its so real, I can feel her there,
alas its in the past, where she cast her spell
The white swan flew low and touched you with
her breast, my swan song, coming out second best.
Everyone knows the rest,
You were left gazing at the moon,
while she followed the sun
Lovestruck and forlorn
in that love tomb.

Oh its been so long since you played
the game of love, now your back in the mix.
The cards are shuffling. the queen of hearts is
waiting, a kaleidoscope of colours,
you just new the hand was yours,
but the dealer dealt a joker
and pinned it to your shirt.

20th Jan 1976

Invisible Threads

When my thoughts become disturbed,
I turn my face to the wall,
staring at blank patterns
of childish innocence,
and wild fired imaginings,
that live and breath
as if alive.

I watch the silver moonbeams
dancing through the door,
spider like, crazying across the floor,
Emptying my mind in puffs of
scented smoke,

The caller is way to late
its check mate.

Outside the earthly zone
everyone is staring at the boy
whose mind is tied with invisible threads,
each thread tells a story,
one for love,
one for pain,
and one for anger,

The thread of love is a chain anchored
to your heart,
The thread of pain hangs waiting to
be pulled.
The thread of anger is tied to love and pain.
And all those who stare have threads of their own.

10th June 1976

Journey of the Philosopher

The philosopher sat at the edge of the forest,
his bony hands upon his lap,
He remembered the passing night,
the cosmic cross embracing the heavens,
he watched and waited for something to unfold,
for a story to be told.
From dusk till dawn, his tired eyes stared toward,
this cosmic spectacle, awaiting some euphoria to land
upon him, he sighed as the sun began to rise,
The heavenly nightscape fading away,
He drifted into a heavy slumber.
She came to him in a dazzling dream,
he was lying on a golden beach,
the years much younger on him,
She shimmered toward him, out of the sun she must have come,
As she sat beside him, the sun moved behind her.
She was light colored, with deep green eyes, like the sea,
who? are you he said,
my kingdom is not all in this world,
he said he heard that line before,
She replied, I have used those words before,
in a time long passed,
he tried to remember, got fleeting feelings of hurt and pain,
she did not show it,
are you eternal, if so show me.
She moved closer to him, wrapping her arms around him,
the world as he new it disappeared, replaced with a feeling

of peace and love. there were colours so vivid
he could not describe them.
there were angels dancing in the sun, he was in a rapture,
basking in some cosmic euphoria, all knowledge
washing over him, in waves of infinity,
her scent was like a garden of flowers.
Who are you he cried out. she released him from the rapture,
he looked into her eyes, he could still see the rolling green
of the sea in them,
She said, what you see is part of me.
I am mother to this earth, and I want you to save her,
How can I do this.
I will show you how ,and I will never be far from you.
She moved away back toward the sun, disappearing, shimmering,
into the distance, his eyes unable to track the marvel of it all.

Part 2

He awoke from the dream, it was mid day,
the sun warm on his back,
The years of age all but gone, once more a young man,
his spirit lifted for the task ahead,
The philosopher now had a purpose,
He left his glade in the forest of uncertainty,
and walked to the meadow, where his journey would begin.
The cosmic cross was introducing the realm of the feminine,
the perfect time to save mother earth,
the divine intervention.

The Philosopher shone like a beacon of light,
preaching to mankind,
showing the errors of their unclean ways,
how they worshipped in the temple of the flesh,
knowing it would age and decay, and turn to dust,
only fragments, particles blowing in the wind.
A greater future awaits you if you worship in the temple
that will open the gates to eternity.
He preached with such passion and purpose, all who truly
listened, went away with opened hearts, that led to changing
ways, that in turn brought them to their changing days,
all for the better, for all of mankind.
The journey of the philosopher spanned forty years,
He travelled all corners of this scorched earth,
ever onwards, beyond boundries,
and the limits of human understanding.
The quest to save mother earth,
The last chance saloon, the final shootout,
dark versus light, good versus evil,
The ultimate fight.

Part 3

Many years further on, the philosopher was walking alone on
a deserted road winding through a desert landscape,
a parched, dry inhospitable place,
He was somewhere near the former city of Jeruselem,
that was now nothing more than rubble and red ash,

enveloping the land, like a torturous hand,
the hand of Armageddon,
the man made hand, that destroyed at least half of this earth,
he had been walking for three days, leaving his followers in
a small village at the edge of this man made hell.
She had told him in yet another dream,
to walk for three days,
keeping the twin suns to his left.
The twin suns had appeared in the sky three days ago, and they
shone with twice the heat, as they rose and set in unison.
The people were terrified, he journeyed on, staff in hand.
An hour or so later, he was overtaken by a savage thirst,
he fell to his knees, beside a large tomb like stone,
he drank from his water bottle, the water almost too hot,
still the thirst, plagued him, the heat was now unbearable.
The suns began to dance across the heavens, one was setting,
the other rising,
His bony hands fluttering, his breath coming in short sharp gasps.
An awful reality bolted in his head, I have failed he thought,
despite every thing, I couldn't save her,
man has destroyed himself,
and the mother earth. hot tears rolled down his face,
rivers of pain,
burning his flesh, he stared at the dancing suns,
archers appeared, shooting arrows of fire across the blinding sky.
His vision was failing, the suns must have damaged his eyes,
it must have been all lies, what a fool he had been,
he was going to die here in this inferno,
that his own kind had made.

Part 4

He sat there in the blistering heat,
his life power almost gone,
why? did you doubt me, he heard her voice,
it was inside his head,
do what I tell you, and do it quickly, he listened,
and did as she asked,
He struggled to his feet, taking with him his flask of water,
he poured the last of the water over the tomb like stone,
and then struck the stone once
with his staff, He fell to the ground,
spinning like a childs top,
When he awoke, the hell heat was gone,
one sun shone alone in a clear blue sky.
The land was covered in a lush carpet of green,
birds were singing,
His vision fully restored, he looked around,
is this the same place surely not,
there was fragments of rock where the larger slab had been,
There was a scent of garden flowers,
that he instantly recognized,
He turned, and looked at heavens gate,
she was there in robes and colours
of such splendour, he was spellbound, I am sorry that I doubted you,
he said in a weak frightened voice.
Her eyes were the same as those he first saw
on the beach of eternity
so long ago, bright and green like the sea.

She came closer to him, and his fear dissolved,
I want to thank you for saving the part of me
that is mother earth,
I am going to reward you, and your followers,
I am giving back to you
this Garden Of Eden,
Which you have paid for with many lifetimes.
a man appeared at her side, he was bearded,
long flowing hair, his clothes
were a brilliant white, his eyes they shone like lights.
A rainbow above him, the colours alive and moving.
He radiated love and peace,
he walked toward the philosopher, reached out
and grasped his hand. the man's hands had old wounds on them,
that were a long time healed, his grip was smooth and strong,
the philosopher felt that this man was all knowing,
a man who was slow to anger, and quick to forgive.
I am the son of man,peace be with you he said.
I wish to bestow upon you my thanks for your service
to my beloved mother. Go now and live in this garden,
I give you my promise,
I will not allow any entity to be responsible for your removal,
This is yours for all that you perceive as time everlasting.

The Garden

The philosopher walked through this garden of colourful splendour,
He noticed a bountiful supply of fruits growing
from trees and bushes
that he had never seen before,
he paused and picked what he thought
was an orange, he bit into the flesh,
it tasted like nothing he had
tasted before, a mixture of orange, chocolate,
and maybe vanilla. It satisfied him.
As he walked on, the years fell away from him,
he was now a young man in his prime,
Time no longer relevant, he continued on.
His body strong and muscular, his stride swift and strong,
He came to a clearing, with a stream running through it,
in the distance he could see a waterfall cascading down
the side of a mountain, the sound wild and wonderful.
There were a number of dwellings scattered about the clearing.
He approached the first mud hut, or was it straw,
he couldn't tell.
A young woman appeared at the entrance,
Welcome she said, I am your guide
I will take you to your dwelling.
In the palace of the righteous.
He followed her across plains,
where wild flowers and grasses all grew
in perfect harmony. bees and butterflies,
and other magnificent creatures,

buzzing and busy, quite content in this garden,
the mother had called Eden.
They travelled on without tiring, each step a new joy,
each sighting a wondrous experience.
A dove of peace flew above them,
an eye in the sky, watching.
The philosopher sensed she would be waiting for him,
his knowledge growing
with every step taken, the longing for her love,
becoming stronger in the
beating of his eternal heart.
He heard her voice rolling across the time span,
he ran to her holding her,
The philosopher had returned home.
Adam she cried I have been alone for so long,
its alright Eve, I am home now for evermore.
The promise has already been made.
the covenant can not be broken,
his word is true.

3rd February 2011 - 9th April 2011.

Lady Midnight

Lady Midnight comes to haunt you,
with her frozen glazed eyes,
she wishes you were a soldier
so she might heal your wounds.

She removes her smile
and lays down upon you,
her arms in a loving embrace,
her body warm and soft as always.

She tells you stories
about other men she's had,
you don't mind listening
but your mind is far away.

Lady Midnight came to haunt you
with her frozen glazed eyes.
I wish I was a soldier
so she might heal my wounds.

2nd Feb 1977

Legacy of a legend

The legacy is handed down through
the generations, in a sacred timeline,
flowing through father and son,
mother and daughter, forever on and
on like a river, through the fertile
plains of life,
oh the pain and the strife,
and the striving to succeed
in this game of skill and speed,
of craft and of guile,
The crack of the ash
as the sliotar flies through the air,
on its flight so true and fair.

There was non swifter,
there was non more gifted,
in the battles, on and off the field,
and in the crusades of the Gael,
Where no one dared to fail.

As he played on the hallowed ground,
all around they watched with wonder.
stricking, clearing, ball after ball.
For club and county, standing tall,
shouting out the battle call.
For forty years he bossed the Faughs
from twenty nine to sixty nine,
a diamond in his own time,

Shining from without and within,
forever driven,
no quarter ever given.
Remembering on this great day,
the leader of our clan,
The legend and the legacy,
That is our Tommy Moore.

On every Patricks day,
when the clubs gather for to play
on the gaels hallowed ground,
With flags and banners all around,
a glorious, tumultous sound,
the clashing of the ash,
echoing through the stands,
and out across the land.

The game is over, the crowd they stand
and cheer. The Tommy Moore is theirs,
The cup is raised aloft,
A proud moment for one and all,
on this great day of the gael,
For wherever you might be.
Even if across the sea.
Raise your glass, and bid adieu,
To the legend and the legacy,
that is our Tommy Moore.

Dedicated to my Grandfather Tommy Moore, and to the Faugh's hurling club, for getting the all Ireland club Championship cup named in his honour. The final which is played in Croke Park on St Patricks Day.
noted. Mick Clayton. Tony Herbert. Eamonn Rea.

30th March 2011

Little One

Oh little one
with your golden hair
you are beautiful.
Oh little one
with baby blue eyes
you are beautiful.
Oh little one
with silver wings,
tiny toes upon the sand
you are beautiful.
Oh little one
with your golden hair,
glistening in the summer sun,
Oh girl, a timeless trance,
a beautiful innocence.

Taken from poems from Love In A Mist.

Nov 1972

Love Remembered

Love is remembered through
dreams of tangerine,
chases and embraces
and soft lips kissing,
the stars up above and
twinkling,
Time burns itself out
through these days of
eternal light.
Personified in a kaleidoscope
of perpetual colours,
that linger through the night.
Love is remembered
through hands touching hands,
on a cold winters night,
where stuttering words plume
in the cold night air
the moment was lost
in that whisp of hot breath.

Love is remembered
through a song,
you watched her sing along,
total focus in a tangerine dream,
caught in a tunnel of time
that must always race painfully
into the dark distant unknown
To sometime be
a love remembered.

25th July 1974

Music

Oh melancholic music
whistling through time,
for music is living
forever giving.
Play play, guitar man
play for her.
Her sweet face forever changing
always young and lovely,
While all around things turn to dust.

Glowing red lips kiss my tongue
and make me feel full.
Your sounds absorb me
your body is warm
and you are so good for me.

Music is moving, drifting soothing,
forever onwards, always embracing
the children of time,
through corridors that seem timeless
an ageless heroine,
For he who made her made me,
in that longing to be free.

Glowing red lips kiss my tongue
and make me feel full
I am lost in your mouth,
your body is warm
and your sounds touch me.

taken from poems from Love In A Mist Nov 72-july 73

Names of Places

Names of places I've never been
places I've never seen,
Between you and me,
theres nothing in between.
Those rolling clouds across
an endless blue horizon.
I have been to you, and you to me,
there's nowhere left to go,
The pictures that are now showing
are of places I have been with you.

Like a child on a train,
gazing through dust stained windows,
seeing for an instant,
just a glimpse of a place he has never been,
of a place he'll say he's seen.

Am I the child in the train
looking at names of places.
its a long time coming,
this work in progress.
As the clouds still roll across
skys of endless blue,
and still those pictures of you.

29th Feb 1980

Night Time Twins

We all walk alone into the slip shod shade
of the night,
leaving the plight of the day, to play in
our heads, until the veil of sleep saves us,
or perhaps derails us. Who? knows,
to each his own. The path unknown.

The street lights watery signature, ghosts
through lace curtains, throwing images across
walls and ceilings that are cracked from father
time and his magic brush, that re paints our
days in his colourful splendour.
eventually fading to grey.

In the dreams of the truth seeker, there lies
unopened doors,
they are shrouded in clouds of uncertainty,
that cling to hands that hold the keys.
The hands are trembling with the fear
of opening a Pandora's box, and witnessing the chaos,
breaking free in the wildest of wreckless wonder.

Walking alone in the dreamscape, upon
a road, that twists toward dawn and the
waiting light, there are figures drifting
in and out of sight, they are threatening,
and maybe hold the key to a menace hidden
in tomorrows unfolding wings.

There are pale faces, now racing toward
the doors, rusted keys held in bony hands,
lights shining, exposing nameless faces,
twin shadows stand before the unopened
doors. The dream ends, there is no answer,
No reason to be concerned,
for the night is long, and we can weave
another dream,
Only this one might make you scream,

In the light of the dawn, the dreamscape
retreats behind unopened doors.
The night Time twins spin to another dimension,
One step beyond the fourth quadrant,
There they wait for another night to unfold.

18th April 2011

Out of Time

Bright lights are shining
burrowing across the heavens,
no one knows what they are,
Some are hovering, some at speed,
their covering up, whats going down.

From Utah to the holy land,
are they beacons of hope,
or symbols of no hope,
eyes gazing, glancing across
endless night skies.

Its a failing world, these pulsing
messages, deciphered by who.
These people in the shadows that
control everything.
parasitic rulers that have bled us
to the bone.
They make the wars to fuel their needs
They want the power to fill their greed.

Mother earth is tortured, raped and pillaged
by the men who sit in ivory towers,
The one World order, is almost here.
Rise up, you people everywhere, and
take back what is yours.
For the fools in the towers,
no not the time or the hour.

The savage winter of twenty ten,
iced over us like a hand of doom,
icicles hung like rapiers in the deepening gloom.
Christmas came through a white veil,
though white, it did not feel right.
Its time to dig deep,
gather your hopes and dreams and hide away
Perhaps in a place of sanctuary,
With loved ones close by, protected.

The winds of change are blowing colder,
they are settling in around your haven,
The piper is standing upright and bold
his hands in a fine neck hold.
your frightened eyes know to well.
Now is the time,
The lights are flickering, in the freezing wind,
Idiots are locked in the Ivory towers,
that are falling, one by one.
The crashing sounds rock your sanctuary,
you can almost see their obituary.
The hand of justice, delivered the crushing blow,
The time is nigh,
for the piper always gets paid.

4th Feb 2011

Pale faced

Pale faced you lie and
your smile is all broken,
here's a gift or a token
which ever you like,
its a ring made of silver
for a child made of gold,
why do I feel so cold.
This love is like a river
racing to the sea.
I'm washed up on the banks
its raining,
your love is draining me,
all these embraces that don't
boomerang back,
leaving me unbalanced,
a one winged eagle
that dreams of soaring high.

The trees drip tears from the sky,
as the night unfolds,
a new moon, and new stars,
in all these things I still see you.
Pale faced you lie and
your smile is all broken.

13th July 1974

Shadows

The shadows that fall upon us as we age,
are not graceful, they are unforgiving,
long and sinewy, sneakily creeping toward you,
With fingers that are sharp, they jab and poke,
in places that time has given up on.
Its a thin line between pleasure and pain,
which side of the line will you sleep on tonight.

The mid day sun casts a small blunt shadow,
reminding you of a child on a sandy beach,
so many things out of reach, in need of time
the teacher, to put your mind in the glowing
and glistening beauty of the sun.

The child of the sun and his shadow are growing
with the day, drifting toward evening and the
lenghtening rays of the ending day,
The long sinewy shadows, are waiting in the dark,
to jab and poke, in places that time has bid goodbye to,

There is no hiding place, the day has died leaving
only fragments of nightlight, trickling through
the windows of your soul, those eyes so blue,
clinging to tomorrows dreams.
The dusk exposing the rust of the day.

The nightime shadows weave their way upon you,
time after time, in a relentless procession,
that jab and poke, always unforgiving.
The shadows always ask.
Which side of the line will you sleep on tonight.
The pleasure or the pain.
There is no answer,
The child of the sun is on the beach, and out of reach,
The teacher is still learning.

22nd January 2011

She

She is the lady in my mind
she is the one I want to love.

In the passionate darkness of
the room,
I can see her, pictured in my mind
Her body lying next to mine,
sky blue eyes that look so kind.

She is the girl that is so fine
the one love forever mine.

I am the prisoner of her body,
she is the keeper of my heart,
You can dance with me,
and hold me in a vice
nice kisses through the night.

She is the lady in my mind,
she is the girl I want to love.

12th May 1976

Sheltered

You could have been the artist,
with word pictures for the world,
following a path to some majestic
mountain.
You did not dare,
for they did not care.
Stopped you in the tracks of time.
The child of the sun hiding in the
shadows of the clouds of reality
raining down shards of glass,
the boy has no class.

The word pictures frozen,
The womb of shelter exposed,
to their expectant dreams,
they had needs, and my dreams
could not feed them.

She told me over and over,
the real world is no place
for pale faced poets who write
about the dawn.
The pawn on the chessboard of life.
Your moves predetermined by the king
and Queen.

Behind the sheltered walls of poetry
hides the dreamy child of the sun.

14th June 1977

Sounds of Silence

Silken sounds through waves of silence
break the bond in my minds eye,
penetrate deeply through the November fog,
Whispering sounds of mellowness bass
embraced as lace, leaving no trace.
Concentration slipping away
when your mind is far away,
far fetched fumbling thoughts
go tumbling on and on.
numbing tired limbs,
rekindling lost memories.
in thoughts of future passed.

Oh silken sounds though waves of silence
Wherefore art thou?
Lost in the November fog,
Sounds of the night,
ship sirens, planes and trains speak
ghostly sounds,
as night creeps toward dawn,
with majestic meaning.
Crave to understand-To understand is all
for the sound of silence catches up on all.

Poems from Love in a Mist 3rd Nov 1972

Sparrow

Sparrow the cat sits on the window ledge
near the edge,
She only fell once, landed and bounced,
carried on regardless.
She watches her world of trees, flying bees
and birds, that are too high in the sky to
bother with.
She basks in the January sun,
but there's no heat in it,
she doesn't care, come summer she knows
all the hotspots,
the cat on the hot tin roof, thats the
garden shed, there she can stalk the magpies
who hang out in the field,
there's one called Peggy who sometimes steals
her cat food. from her bowl on the patio,
Then there's the spot between the bamboos,
great for cat napping on warm sunny days.

Sparrow the cat doesn't care much for how
the economy is doing, or how the politicians
plan to proceed.
There's no cool cats in politics she purrs.
She knows two cool cats at the top of the road,
Luke and Kelly, she sometimes hangs out with them,
they play cat tag, she says they cheat, and comes
home to sulk in her box beside the radiator.

Sparrow the cat hates, fur balls, rain, thunder,
and those windy days, that blow her all over
the place, she doesn't like sudden movements either,
and she can trip you, while she's waiting to be fed.
She doesn't mean to, she just does.
Sparrow the cat rocks ,and she knows it.

Written for Kevin age 13. 24th Jan 2011

Sugar on a Tight Rope

She came through the evening
with her stardust painted face,
wearing lace, your arms reaching
for her sacred embrace.
She danced to the beat of my heart,
Stole it, and left me standing alone,
in the after glow of her multi coloured
aura.

Sugar's on her tight rope, but I'm
the one thats falling.
Oh lady you are my amber light,
love me through the foggy night.

She danced and tip toed around the
thoughts in my head,
slipped out through the magic hidden
door, out and under the moon, with my
heart upon her sleeve, and my cold lips
shivering in the warm shelter of love
in a mist, and the music played on.

Sugar's on a tight rope, but your the
one thats falling,
oh lady you are the most,
hold me close,
oh lady you are my amber light,
Love me through the foggy night.

The evening closes out, the dance floor
is empty, Her scent lingers on, musk, and jade.
or something hot and spicy,
lots of tongue twisting images
of her stardust painted face,
in my head, gone without a trace.

Oh lady you are the most,
release me from this tomb,
and free me in your womb.
Oh lady you are my amber light
guide me through the foggy night.

Sugar's on her tight rope.
but I'm the one thats falling.

5th November 1975

Sweet Solitude

The rain pattered on the window pane,
dulling the love pain,
that floated above and beyond me,
it danced and spun, like a halo
on some forgotten saint.
Sweet Solitude she said,
you could have tried harder,
your love for me was half hearted.
drifting on, a spiral, stuck in a groove,
a broken record.
Rock'n rolling with the crowd,
I'm bowing out.
Words that cut to the bone.
I reached for the phone,
she told me not to.

Oh sweet solitude,
are you all thats left to me,
my only friend.
She was everything to me
flesh and bone,
my beating heart.

The rain pattered on the window pane.
No pain no gain, some fool said,
The love sick child still felt the dulling pain
and watched in wonder at the never ending rain.

18th October 1976

Switched Off

Sitting in a crowded room
voices all around.
like arms, strangling my thoughts,
All the somebodies and all the
nobodies, struggling for a word
in a conversation about nothing.

There's music playing, the voices
are too loud, its crowded out,
I think its Jackson Browne,
singing For a Dancer.
The girl in the corner of my eye,
smiles,
Her eyes are sad like mine.

The evening drags on,
the players come and go,
the lights fade to blue,
pale faces, ghostlike images
moving to and fro.
The sound of music, drifts on
waves of scented incense.

Outside a siren sings,
Outside I get some air.
When I return.
the girl with the sad eyes is gone.
This timespan is trickling to a close.
Its one in hindsight, I would not have chose.
The music switches off.

August 1976

The Bitter and the Sweet

She sits on the edge of her tomorrows,
her eyelids toward the sun,
hiding a vacant void, in her once sunny
blue eyes,
Her world of yesterdays, whirl and spin
with an unsettling uneasy feeling,
like a roller coaster ride,
thats going off the rails.
The voice in her head is shouting,
I told you so, thats all it ever says.
When life's labels become difficult to read,
she withdraws to the windowless room,
in the dark corner of her mind,
its there all things are overseen,
placed in order on her silver screen.

Oh the bitter and the sweet of it,
those triumphs and defeats,
anchored together, in a mystical place,
tethered in a storm,
the tension painted in lines upon her face.
red lips pouting, only to sip from another
poisoned chalice.

The ocean that her life has floated on,
has become a dark and stormy place,
the birds of prey are hovering,
above this lonely child.
She remembers the days of the sweet rain,
there she new no pain, but that was long ago,
before the bitter and the sweet,
and the taste of life that soured her.

In the corner of her eyes,
the angel of love is standing,
he's shooting arrows across her field
of vision, he points to her tethered feet,
her head rolls forward, staring at the twin chains
one disappearing into the earth,
the other floating towards the heavens.
I can free you from only one, he sighed,
you must make the call,
The earthly chain, she cried, free me now,
she feels the chain loosen and fall away,
into a grinding earth,

Oh the bitter and the sweet of it,
through the triumphs and defeats,
no longer anchored,
no longer tied, to earths painful woes,
Her past played out on the silver screen,
in the room where no one was allowed to go.

She's sitting near the waters edge,
its calm and peaceful.
Her long blond hair flowing in a gentle breeze,
her sunny blue eyes, alive with the knowing,
what was lost is now found,
a cloud in the shape of a cherub angel,
passes overhead,
she looks up and smiles.
oh the bitter and the sweet of it,
the journey is now complete.

21st April 2011

Box Of Images

The portal thats now open, is one not seen
through out the years of wandering blindly
along desert landscapes, towns and cities,
where only the hooded people lived,
for thats all they were to you,
before you climbed outside the box.

In the boxes where people live,
there are confinements,
limitations put in place, to keep others out,
and to keep your little snout in line.
Closed narrow little minds,
watching dumb down TV,
No idea or concern about whats really going on,

The box people dine on processed junk,
food and pills alive with toxic chemicals,
their bodies under constant attack,
on the road to oblivion. The Watchers watching,
from towers along the horizon.

The limits of life in the box,
create stagnant mind sets,
that move in ever diminishing circles,
casting shadows old and grey,
never wanting to be shown the way.
seeing only their way through rose tinted glasses,
that may as well be black.

Feeble arms and legs totter from
the TV room to the kitchen,
back and forth, hands clutching
the TV remote. the push button world,
is always open for the business of fools.

In the box, lives live in sheltered confusion,
eyes bleary eyed, from meaningless war games,
the soldiers killed repeatedly, but never die,
how real is that, no one notices, the virtual battle continues,
the hours whittle by, another day gone.
Lost to the land of shadows.
Outside the box, the sun shines, the rain falls,

The enquiring mind is always open, reaching outside
the limits of the I want more box, or the, I'm part of the
jet set box, both eventually self destructing, in a spectacular
is this all there is, meltdown.(more pills required)
I can reach out to you, I can teach you something new,
and you might do the same for me, but the walls are high,
the limits of existence controlled from another realm.

The puppet masters have you dancing the wrong moves,
with the steps you choose, you can only lose.
People projecting images of who they want you to see,
you never see the real deal, its hidden behind a facade
of false props,

The three piece suit, the designer this, or the I have that,
and the must have current zero year car,
status symbol brand only.

These projected images play to the crowd from within the box,
the dwellers frantically pushing the buttons that make them tick.
Behind the images are frightened faces,
that feed on the status these
projections bring.
Careful choreographed actions, balanced with a smooth
storyline that tells you nothing,
This delicate house of cards is the perfect
illusion, weaving through lives,
lived in the constraints of a box.

Deep inside the box, the mind reels are turning,
churning up more images
to blind the unwary,
the controls on the panels are burning hot.
The smoke funnelling up in circles, stinging,
tearing eyes that have
seen enough. The images are failing,
the props collapsing all around.
The box flies open.
Inside a small child like creature sits,
tiny hands clinging to a remote
control, a multitude of screens hiss white noise.

The box dweller continues to push the buttons,
the sceens remain blank.
On the far side of the universe, the controller watches
as the boxes begin to open,
he pushes the off switch, shuts down the power,
Experiment failed.
Another world lost.
A report is filed.

25th April 2011

The Empty chair

The leader of our band is gone,
I sit and stare at the empty chair,
looking for answers to a question
no one gets to hear.
The book with many pages unread,
left for the undead.
The unpaid bills with your familiar name,
It feels unreal, like a game.
I can never win.
Sad faces, blood shot eyes, why?
Her face turns to you and cries.
The twisting and the turning,
of memories that are burning,
Fading back, only to attack,
again and again.
How brutal it is when love is taken
from you, leaving you cold and empty,
on a crisp October morn,
No real warning, for such a calling.
A lifetime gone in a moment,
but painted forever on the screen
at the back of you mind,
to be played over and over
in an endless loop,
Where your fingers fumble in a futile dance,
for the off switch,
but the power is always on.

You cant fill the empty chair,
you will not read those unread pages,
I can't cut the cord thats tied to you.
The window of pain is open,
its blowing in waves of cold,
over memories of gold,
These brittle bones are somehow
rattling on, the mystery still a puzzle.
I look to the light, for the peace,
that might set me free,
or let me be.
and for the wisdom ,and understanding,
not to try and fill the empty chair.

for Dad who died 23rd October 2006

The Searcher

I've been looking for a long long time,
for my sea of blue so calm,
but all the time the waves are high,
I can only look with sighing eyes.

I've been walking for a long long time,
on this road that might take me where
I want to be, but it seems to go in circles,
all I get is around, never to be found.

I've been listening for a long long time
to the music I call my own,
but in all this time the songs all sound
the same, its another losing game.

I've been searching for a long long time
for a girl who might like to love me,
in the blue room she held my embrace,
then left without a trace.

On the outskirts of his imagination,
the searcher is moving slowly,
the past close by and moving too.
The road is dark and misty,
he can't afford to miss this time.

In the dawn's early light, the grey
mist is clearing, the road ahead seems
long and empty, the searcher continues,
the three dimensions of time move close by,
past. present, and future,
In all of these the searcher seeks.

23rd September 1974. 22nd April 2011

This Old 55

The cold steel sky
refused to celebrate
this old 55,
its radiating dampness
permeated through out my day,
31st DEC 55 is now fifty five.
The mirror angles and sways,
as if to say go away.

You put your best foot forward,
ever onward to meet the day
Cell phone chiming hotel California,
another new years wish,
another year filed to the past.
its a message on the virtual highway,
it reads,
Life may not be the party we hoped for,
but while we are here we should dance.
Happy new year, from uncle Joe.
The Christmas lights still twinkling.
the child of the sun still wondering,
thoughts still jumbling along.
this old 55 is rattling on.
Now where's those dancing shoes.

31st December 2010

Thread from the past

Nothing haunts the present like memories from the past
Those perfect endless days, were they ever really there,
thoughts that roam your mind are not all that kind.
The images of her are bleeding colours in your mind.
She's a thread from the past, tugging at fragile feelings
that should be left alone. She's a time bomb,
A once fine wine, gone off with the ravages of time.
A sunken wreck, waiting to be refloated.
If so, will drift once again on to the rocks,
of your shallow harbour.

On the other side, the real sun is shining,
Rainbow colours spinning and shimmering,
twilight pinks and oranges bathed in beauty
to be or not to be, lets just let it be
the thread from the past is hanging,
If I pull it will it set me free.

The girl from the past is the thread.
She has become a noose around my neck,
In dreams of fire she turns away,
the knot is tightening,
the face is turning pale.

The memories are mind movies,
poised to play, when present days
become tiresome, and the illusion
of the perfect past, deserves one last
blast.
The wreck is refloated, she's sailing across
two decades, to once again drift on to
the rocks of your shallow harbour.

4th June 1985

Time the Illusion

All these days that are spent
finding time, spending time,
racing along your track,
faster and faster,
as the cracks start to appear,
papered over with time spent away.

Time is an illusion, the best ever.
twenty years of never,
where did it go,
it went in boring Mondays
and dreamy Sundays,
little of it recalled
when required.

I can still see days lost in times of
childhood games, a small boy in a
garden of flowers, a scent of blossom
on a warm summers day,
gone in an instant,
along with all the other yesterdays,
floating on rivers of memories,
tied only to you, and you alone.
To be viewed in darker times,
when the summers are colder,
and your dreams are locked into
the pause mode.

Times illusion rocks me back to my
present days, to be greeted by my own
reality, which mockingly says
I once was young, but not anymore
I once was, and time will say is no more.

2nd August 1992

Tombs of Ice

High poised romantic charm,
lies hidden behind cobwebs of simple fear
Nothing better to do but sit and watch,
while the dancing songbirds chatter religiously
about the downfall of Mr Majestic.

During lunch hour when the day is
perfectly balanced,
She asks you questions that
you don't know the answers to,
She laughs, and leaves.
A shadow moving,
leaving you cold and numb
in the November sun.

Later on when the frost has kissed
the earth with icy lips,
the once green leaves lie firmly frozen
in tombs of ice.
insane memories of people dancing
in the shadows of my mind,
each dancer burdened with a smile

The dancing songbirds are silent,
their songs encased in tombs of ice.

30th Nov 1976

Too high a price

I've been here too long,
playing games in my head
acting out parts of heroes,
where all my roles
lead to zeros.
Singing pale songs while
strumming along.
I'm on the high wire
waiting to fall from my
high lofty thoughts.
They go around in
a spiral, to end at the same
place as they began,
they crystallise and remain stagnant
only to pitter on hopelessly toward nowhere.
The sounds of emptiness echo and
re echo off the walls of my mind,
Leaving me paying to high a price
for something I never had.

15th Nov 1975

Trampled

The sun is shining through the tinted
shades of Autumn.
the leaves like flames blow around me,
the beauty of nature astounds me.
Here in the primrose days of my life,
the days roll along to the beat of the songs,
the meaning unfolding in the wisdom of words
that play and replay from day to day,
showing me the way.

I feel like a soldier of fortune,
struggling to survive on fading dreams,
and a distant love story, that remains captured
on the endless waves of emotional tides
that rise and fall, on this Autumn day.
The leaves are burning flaming colours,
smoke beginning to blind pale blue eyes.
the path has become twisted.
I stumble into a clearing,
breathing faint scents of old smoke,
life has become such a joke.

The people with wooden doors
will not open them.
The people with coloured doors
pretend not to see you
The people with long drives
lock the gates.

Here in the silver days of the sun,
the rabbit hides his head,
all alone and trampled.

22nd Sept.1976

Uncle Franks day

Started off early on that Sunday morn',
a west wind blowing cold across the midlands,
deserted towns in squally showers, brief pictures
passing by, on a January day.
The radio on, just killing time.
Onward bound, on a winding road,
from Tullamore to old Kilcormac,
a point along the western way,
on our journey down, for Uncle Frank's day.

In the pale winter sun we huddled around,
sorry for your trouble,
its a happy release,
words that don't mean much when death's in town.
the tolling of the bell in the icy wind played
a cold lonely tune, to remind us of our own mortality,
which is always only a heartbeat away,
nothing is revealed to us in this earthly realm.
Everything hangs above us, enveloping like a shroud.
As we gather here together on Uncle Frank's day.

We stood in the cemetery frozen with cold and fear,
winter faces that are lost in the wilderness of pain,
and anguish, a legacy that death leaves us with,
Out of the sadness a robin appears, he hops, and bops
about the open grave,
A gift from the heavens, a sign of hope, of comfort,

perhaps a sign, that this end is a new beginning.
that in this present time we can find no trace of.

I'll always remember our robin, when times gentle breeze,
takes me back to Uncle Frank's day.
I have fond memories of childhood days,
football in the garden with our country cousins,
and Uncle Frank watching, his pipe gently puffing,
a father enriched by what his children might be.
In years to come the dreams came true.
What more can one ask for,
I thought of all these things
on Uncle Frank's day.

I wish you all well,
I thank you for your kindness.
Although I spoke to few.
I felt enriched, a part of,
for that I'm grateful.

As I sat in that bright kitchen,
amidst relatives from far and near,
I guess just being there was the best
I could do,
I'm glad I went all that way
for Uncle Frank's day.

Dedicated to Frank Currums , Ella Currums, Eileen Moore
22nd January 1993

Unfinished Times

The sundial moving on its way, bestowing upon time
an illusion of being a slow moving entity,
Its deception, ringing through the decades,
like a loud locomotive, looming into a fragile
future, that beckons with open arms,
waiting to embrace these unfinished times.

The Shadowmen move their armies across vast
plains, like pieces on a chess board,
the victors and the vanquished, sharing the
spoils of death, those sacred battlefields,
forever named, Gettysburg, Waterloo, Little big
Horn, The Somme, the list is an endless litany,
of man's lust for power, through the force of a brute,
and the blinding failure to see the futility of its truth,
as its played out over and over again ,and the lives lost,
despatched to the heavens in the bloody moments,
of these unfinished times.

Loved ones left on the fringes of what life might
have been, if the shadowmen had come clean,
what if they cared, and not dared,
what if they shared, maybe a different shadow,
might have been cast upon us.
The terrible ego's of men gone mad,
a tyranny on ones own people,
cast down with a ruthlessness, that cannot and will not

be understood, by future generations looking
back with angry disbelieving eyes,
the tears streaming down, through the years
that have led them to these unfinished times.

Oh what did you see young man, on the field
of war, what did you feel, as the bullets flew,
and the bayonets stabbed and pierced fragile flesh,
in this futile dance of death,
I thought only of love he said,
the ones at home in the sun,
that I may never see again.
War is a virus, a plague, that has meandered down
though time, more virulent with the passing years,
each generation enslaved, to the early grave,
Was there not enough love in the world,
to end the hate, can we even begin to speculate,
our journeys end, through these unfinished times.

The shadowmen are standing on the edge of their
own abyss, their clammy hands wrapped around the
puppet strings. the armies fallen. the flags unfurled,
the nuclear wind of change, pushing them closer to the edge,
the dimension of loss feeds through them,
empty eyes devoid of understanding,
the angel of justice finally stands above them,
his sword for humanity drawn,
its delivery is swift,
the mad men despatched, moving onward
in these unfinished times.

The sundial spins a new day,
the time that is now, trickles on,
to meet with the waves of infinity,
The shadowmen are moving across
the endlessness of space,
watching, waiting, controlling.
Their bony little fingers pointing
to the sun. The dial is moving forward,
the watcher watching,
the pieces unmoving on the board.
each piece chained to the thread
of unfinished times.

13th April 2011

The Weary Travellers Of The World

Take the sleep from your eyes,
oh you weary traveller of the world,
tell me your sorrows
so that I might borrow.

I just need a lover,
someone I can relate to,
a non taker, a free spirit,
to dust these cobwebs,
then let me be.

Pretty Easter morning,
the sun is in the sky,
the long cold winter
has unfolded,
you are free to hunt again.

Its a funny kind of feeling
when time goes by without meaning,
but its like that all the time
for the weary travellers of the world.

19th October 1976

Who's Jennifer

Just dropped in with carnations
and wine,
to talk about Jennifer and the
emulsion of colours in her very
fine mind.
Play the music softly
she likes it so.
I'm only the singer with so many songs
and she's part of a song I keep getting wrong.
I've been searching so long,
but the words don't belong.
These feelings of love
are so very strong
I can feel her so close
its not what I chose.

Time spins in a spiral of sound,
around and around,
feet way off the ground.
Theres pink and theres mauve
made of jelly delight.
Who switched on the light
where's the soft music.

I look around an empty room
the carnations are withered
and Jennifer is dead in my head,
the wine was just to fill a line.

Taken From Mystic Moments, 13th July 1974

Heroes And Villains

As we weave our way though this journey,
on down life's winding road, sometimes we pause
as the waves come crashing on our
fragile dreams,
or when the walls are closing in,
We have threads to cling to,
graces to lift us up, to once more
drink from life's plentiful cup.

Life is littered with stations,
where you step on and step off,
at each station there are heroes and villains.
here they wait for your hungry thirst.
Childhood stations have super heroes,
Superman, Spiderman, and Batman.
The villains, were much more fun.
As life moves on the heroes are more
complex, the villains far more sinister.

We are all influenced by others,
seeking their own path,
their talent, skill, and spirituality,
racing down this information highway
to be soaked up by our inquiring minds,

As a tribute to those who have
helped me drink from the cup of life.
for those, who have brought me to the water,
To those heroes, who's presence inspired a belief,
to reach out and hold the dream, that may have
otherwise slipped through trembling hands,
and be lost in the tunnell of regret,
never to be seen or heard by anyone.

I salute them, on this platform,
from this station that I'm now at, and
this creation, thats in this finite time,
If there is but one line,
in all I've written that makes you stop and think
The journey will not have been wasted.
May some of my heroes be yours too.

IN NO PARTICULAR ORDER

God, Jesus Christ, creator, without whom there would
be nothing at all. I am.
Mam and Dad,
for giving more than anyone should have had to.
Dale Carnegie, for life changing books and courses,
Norman Vincent Peale----for the power of positive thinking.
Alan Freeman-----for pick of the pops, Greetings pop pickers.
John Peel,----English DJ who played stuff no one else would.
Larry Gogan------for playing pop music in the sixties on
rte radio sponsored shows,
Johnnie Walker. First heard the Eagles on his BBC radio one
lunch time prog. (Pop the Question.) 70s.
Stephen King-----for the Stand , first King book I read.
Have read them all.
Michael Connolly----for Harry Bosche.
Lee Childs--------for Jack Reacher.
Joseph O Connor.-----Ghostlight, Star of the Sea.
Radio Luxembourg-----when there was nothing else
The Monkees-------first pop heroes 1966/67
John Lennon-------Imagine. Working Class Hero.
John Fogarty-------for Creedence Clearwater Revival.
Jackson Browne------for the Pretender, lives in the balance.
the rebel Jesus. One of the best Singer Songwriters,
I have listened to. lyrics way beyond his years,
back in the 70s.big influence.
Dan Fogelberg-----For the Leader of the band, sutters mill.
longer, and so much more. Dan has a truly amazing angelic voice,
hugely under rated artist. Sadly missed. Love his music and lyrics.

Steely Dan-----amazing music, katy lied, do it again,
hey nineteen, Hatian Divorce.etc
Neil Diamond----Hot August Night 1972.
plus all his other Diamonds.
Carole King-----Tapestry.
Carly Simon-----No secrets, you're so vain.
Clint Eastwood-----The man with no name, Dirty Harry,
The Outlaw Josey Wales, Clint was my all American
hero from Rawhide to Gran Torino.
and every thing in between. Great Director as well.
The Beach Boys,-----for all that summer music.
Ian Fleming -----James Bond.
Neil Young, -------for Harvest, and his version of
four strong winds. and Crazy horse
Jim Croce,------for Time in a Bottle, I got a name, etc,
died in a plane crash in 73.
Bruce Springsteen for Born To Run,Darkness
On The Edge Of Town, Somebody wrote back in 1975
Bruce Sprinsteen is the future of Rock N Roll,
they were right.
Don Mclean------American pie, Vincent.
Eagles-----for Desperado, I played that record,
until it wore out in the 70s.
thanks to the Eagles for eventually playing Ireland.
seen all the shows. all time favourite band.
Long Road out of Eden, great biblical album.
Glenn Frey---Strange Weather,
and playing and filming his show at the National Stadium
in 1992.great show.

Don Henley-----for vocals on the Eagles albums,
and for his own solo work, ie Inside Job etc
Randy Meisner----for Take it to the limit, amazing vocals.
Bernie Leadon ------For My Man.
from Eagles album On The Border,
one of my favourite songs.
Bob Seeger, for Nightmoves, Main Street,Hollywood Nights.
Leonard Cohen ------Wonderful poet songwriter.
an absolute legend. So long Marianne.
Tower Of Song, Closing Time, Hallelujah, etc
The list is endless.
Richard Harris-----For McArthur Park,
great Jimmy Webb song.
Harris is great on it. Great actor as well.
Bob Geldof------Live Aid, for being a true human being,
no one else could have done it.
Mother Teresa-----for giving everything a life could give.
Fr. Arthur O'Neill, Fr. Tom O'Keefe, Fr. Conor Ward,
Cabinteely Parish, for support during trying times.
Johnny Cash------Dad loved him, Walk The Line,
Ring Of Fire, Forty Shades Of Green. for Mam.
Gay Byrne------for the meaning of life.
Great people on it, great questions.
Gerry Ryan------for not being the same as everybody else
on the radio, (empty spaces are hard to fill)
David Icke.------- for thinking outside the box.
A very interesting man, worth checking out on you tube.
Mike Adams, The Health Ranger---
for Naturalnews.com, thanks for all the health tips and links,
a beacon of light in an increasingly darkening world,

long may you run.
Dr.Mark Sircus,---for transdermal magnesium therapy,
iodine, sodium bicarbonate, natural healer supreme,
one of gods shining lights.
Dr.Joseph Mercola, Natural healer,
great products and a passion for healthy living
and for sharing it with all.
Cat Stevens.---for great albums in the early 70s,
Teaser and the Firecat, Tea for the Tillerman,
Catch Bull at Four.
Jon Barron ----for Lessons from the Miracle doctors,
everyone should read it.
Dr. Jonathan Wright, Tahoma clinic Washington,
-----for there is another way to heal,
without being poisened. pioneer of alternative medicine.
Mike Oldfield------Tubular Bells.
Horslips------------Progressive Irish music.
Elvis-----King of Rock and Roll.
Phil Lynott-------Best Irish rocker,
The Boys Are Back In Town.
Jack Charlton-----Irelands quest for soccer glory.
Ole Ole Ole. best manager, best team.88.90.94.
Pete Ryan-------best friends since 4 years of age,
still meet every week for a pint.
Mr Craven English teacher Oatlands .for ------
Music is the highest form of art, loved that,
Gerry McGarry -----
local singer songwriter, for never giving up.
Clifford T Ward for Gaye and other stories.
Dublin City Ramblers-----

for ballads at the lower deck in the 70s.
Luke Kelly----for Raglan Road and the Dubliners.
Gordon Lightfoot.---Canadian singer songwriter,
ie Sundown, Wreck of the Edmund Fitzgerald,
If you could read my mind. Early Morning Rain.
Bono----U2,---making the world a better place,
Africa etc etc. Could just as easily have done nothing.
Bill Clinton-------Helping bring peace to Ireland,
put us on the international stage.
Kris Kristofferson.----Great songwriter.
Sunday Morning Coming Down,One Day at a Time,
Me and Bobby Magee.
Ennio Morricone.---Italian composer, movies,
spaghetti westerns, The Good, The Bad And The Ugly
plus many more.
Sergio Leone---- Italian film director.
the Dollar films with Clint Eastwood.
Jack Nicholson------for One Flew Over The Cuckoos Nest.
Rolling Stones----for Brown Sugar, Jumping
Jack Flash,Satisfaction, Angie. etc.
Status Quo-----for air guitars, headbanging in the 70s.
Deep Purple-----for Smoke on the Water. Machine Head.
holidays in France in 72
Black Sabbath---Paranoid, vol 4.Changes.
Mungo Jerry------In The Summertime.
Jimmy Saville. pioneer disco dj and top of the pops.
Led Zeppelin-----Rock n roll, black dog, stairway to heaven.
The Who-----for my generation. wont get fooled again.
Paul Rodgers---for Free, and Bad Company
Queen-----for Freddie Mercury, great singer, great songs.

Simon and Garfunkel---for Bridge Over Troubled Water,
Sound Of Silence, Scarborough Fair.
Dj Rob Moore-------dedicated to the cause,
and hotspot events. Techno dj extraordinaire.
Siobhan Moore---Wife and mother, who puts up with a lot,
never complains?
John Moore ------Eldest son, great student,
dedicated sports fan
Kevin Michael Moore---youngest of the gang,
another DJ, maybe.
Fr's Michael and Kevin Doheny.
for missionaries beyond the call of duty.
Al Stewart,-------for Modern Times, Year of the Cat,
Bob Dylan.------artistic legend from the 60s,
right through to today
Glam rock stars from the 70s.Marc Bolan, T.rex. Slade,
The Sweet, Mud, Alvin Stardust. etc. leo Sayer.
Liverpool football greats 70s and 80s.
5 times European cup winners. Bill Shankly Bob Paisley,
Joe Fagan. Kenny Daglish, Ian Rush, Emlyn Hughes,
Kevin Keegan, The baton handed on.
You'll Never Walk Alone.
Mick o'Connell. Kerry fooball legend from the 60s.
Ned Malone. One of the truly nicest people I ever met.
(UNCLE)
Jim Morrisson, The Doors, for Riders On The Storm ,
L.A. Woman, The End. Jim was once asked what he would
like to be remembered for he said the Words man the Words.

David Wolfe---- for cutting edge nutrition and health
technologies, and for his longevity programme,
medicinal mushrooms, Reishi, Chaga. another wonderful
natural health advocate. great audio and visual programmes,
filled with great info. keep on zapping.
Sir Alex Ferguson-----coming from a Liverpool fan.
everyone could learn something from him.
Bryan Holland (Dutch) Buddies from times long gone,
but not forgotten.
The Bellevue Park kids,------great place to grow up in,
great friends, love in a mist disco, 72--2003.
Darts and Snooker Tuesday nights,
right through the 80s and 90s,

Villians

The politicians, greedy bankers and developers who wrecked this little country. recent political parties--for providing no leadership whatsoever, and failing the citizens of this state, with weak and inept government

The arrogant governments world wide, who lie to their people, about what's really going on,(massive abuse.) and who stick their vested interested little fingers in every ones pie, and tell you its all for world peace, don't believe a word, control, control, thats all that matters, enough said.

The massive pharmaceutical juggernaut, that controls all aspects of health, and spits out its poisenous coktails of toxic drugs, in a massive deception programme, that's powered by money, sacred cash cows, at the expense of our health, be informed, take charge of your own health. Good luck with that.

P.S. Could not have completed this project without some input from most of the above, some more so than others.

May whatever force or guiding light you believe in, be forever with you.

Brian Moore
Unfinished Times.2011